Gut Sandwich

Why Gap Analysis Falls Short and Doesn't Tell the Whole Story.

Kevin S. Crowder, CEcD, EDP

Copyright © 2023 Kevin S. Crowder

All rights reserved

No part of this book may be reproduced, or stored in a retrieval system, or transmitted in any form or by any means, electronic, mechanical, photocopying, recording, or otherwise, without express written permission of the publisher.

BusinessFlare® Publishing Group

Cover design by Lina M. Duque

Printed in the United States of America

ISBN: 9798862418217

The commonly understood type of gap analysis is insufficient as it only considers one factor and does not consider the intangible of the entrepreneur's potential. Many other factors affect a business's ability to serve all kinds of demand, and some businesses and entrepreneurs can compete and succeed in an oversupplied sector. Gap analysis occurs when a community's downtown offerings are often different from what people want. But true success lies in creating a place people want to be with what they want. That is the realm of the entrepreneur not the analyst. If downtowns do not have what people want, downtowns must figure out why people do not want to provide those things in their community.

Ultimately, successful economic development is an exercise in intestinal fortitude and not always a place to play it safe. Look beyond the trailing data and find your community's potential. Learn from successful entrepreneurs and apply their thinking to your economic growth efforts. Don't rely solely on the data; instead, put the relevant data between a slice of intuition and a slice of instinct and eat a Gut Sandwich.

So, there are a few examples of how you start finding stories. Once you find one, you start pulling on the threads, and more stories emerge. They start weaving together into a story of entrepreneurship, success, opportunity, and potential. So, as you think about the stories from a new perspective of placemaking Economic Design™ rather than just stories to enjoy around the table, find the right people in places to tell these stories to and get to work.

Contents

Introduction 1

Potential Matters, Not Demand 3

Investment Drivers 7

Community Connections 14

Customers 16

Gap or Gut? 21

Opportunities 25

Economic Design™ 34

Tell Your Stories 38

Special thanks to the Flareheads™ for support and overall awesomeness and making this book, and everything we accomplish, possible.

Alicia Alleyne
Camilo Lopez
Stacy Kilroy
Peter Altman
Link Walther
Julio Magrisso
Rachel Bach
Charita Allen
Ken Stapleton
Allison Justice
Kent Bonde
Julian Duque
Lina Duque

Acknowledgements

The BusinessFlare® Academy is a not-for-profit Economic Development Corporation that was created to provide realistic economic development education and training for local government officials, which is focused on understanding successful implementation and outcomes.

Too often local governments focus on economic development tactics without a strategy, seemingly throwing things against the wall waiting for something to stick. And equally too often economic development training avoids the uncomfortable realities of day to day implementation.

Through a series of training sessions, one-on-one and organizational retreats, online webinars, and eBooks, we can provide a base of understanding that helps local governments implement strategies that can improve their local economy and grow their tax base within the limitations of their resources.

Proceeds of the sale of this book will benefit the BusinessFlare® Academy.

"Not everything that counts can be counted, and not everything that can be counted counts."
-Albert Einstein (according to the internet)

1
Introduction

This work is not only about market analysis, it is about storytelling. It is about market potential and opportunity, not market demand because, you see, market demand is only an analysis that makes you look at the past and what that means is you're just looking at data that tells you how you got to a place that maybe you don't want to be anymore. It does not have to have anything to do with where you can go, or your potential.

And so what we're talking about when we talk about market potential is we're talking about stories. Those are things you cannot measure but which are more critical than inanimate numbers. And very importantly, we will talk about stories of things you can't measure.

And so, when it comes to market analysis and market research data, especially for small organizations without resources, it can sometimes be overwhelming and sometimes feel a little lost. I was the economic development director for Miami Beach for a long time. And even in Miami Beach, I lacked the financial resources for the systems and the data I wanted to access. So, I had to find ways to bootstrap it. We can access the free data from the Census and look at the Economic Census. Now, the problem is that those things need to catch up, and you don't even start seeing the results of that data for two years. We can track labor and the quarterly Census of wages at the state, but we only get that at the county level. We can follow some sales tax stats, which we also get at county level.

I made sure I was friends with real estate brokers who would feed me MLS and commercial real estate data from Costar™. I was good friends with our Convention and Visitor's Bureau to ensure I got good tourism survey data. And we collected a resort tax, which was our best data since it was something that lagged only about six weeks. But you know, we were building this program ourselves. And we were creating innovative ways to do our analysis. There are many different ways to try and use data because that is one of the significant needs that our investors, developers, and businesses have; it's something they want. We built a robust municipal market research with the data and analysis.

But people also wanted the stories.

2
Potential Matters, Not Demand

When we started talking about the South Beach experience, we started getting questions about how South Beach happened. The longer we considered it, we realized that it was the potential, not market demand. It was market potential. It was opportunity.

In the '70s and early '80s, South Beach and Ocean Drive were known as God's Waiting Room. In 1982, the Miami Herald published a 12-page special called "South Beach, Where Dreams Die." This is the neighborhood where Brian DePalma shot the chainsaw scene from Scarface at a building that only a few years later became the Irene Marie modeling agency.

SOUTH BEACH
WHERE DREAMS DIE

A MIAMI HERALD SPECIAL REPORT

by MICHAEL KRANISH

Photography by Bill Frakes

But Ocean Drive was different in 1982. In the mid-80s, when Tony Goldman and others came down from New York and looked at Ocean Drive, he saw the blight, saw it in South Pointe even further south on the island a few blocks away where there was a development moratorium, because that neighborhood was going to be one of the most significant urban renewal projects in the country.

There was no market analysis, and no demand study could have guided what came next, or that would have said that Tony and the other folks who came in could succeed at what they did.

They would create the Ocean Drive we came to know as this great place that people want to be, one of America's best public spaces. I couldn't have done a hotel demand analysis for that. And you couldn't have done a sidewalk cafe analysis, as sidewalk cafes weren't even allowed in the city's code. But there was the potential. He saw the place, and he saw the architecture. He said I can do this and thus became the realization of all of that potential.

So, I will walk you through some of the data, and then we'll get into the stories. And we'll talk about not just South Beach because I know a lot of the times the South Beach example can feel unrelatable, and one of the things we've spent much time on both in my time in Miami Beach and especially since is to take that lesson and to make it relatable, which we've done in about 60 communities over the last 11 or 12 years. But I'm going to give you examples from those communities. I will tell you the story of how we came up with this approach and the importance of those stories. I will tell you examples, some of which are more significant than you can accomplish and others much less. But they can sometimes have these audacious results, and you catch that genie in the bottle.

And so we want to understand the condition in your downtown, of your community, about the different things that drive investment, the economy, and the markets. I have meetings with elected officials to review our data findings, examine the feasibility or feasibility of different options, and give them a respectful reality check about what they can and can't do in the numbers. Because we're not just going to talk about the data that we find. We will talk about how you look at feasibility and how you have to use an approach that is not only economic development but rather Economic Design™.

3

Investment Drivers

So we will talk about that towards the end. But back to the investment drivers. Six things; it used to be three, and we added two, and we recently added a sixth. Land, Labor, and Capital are taught as the three things that drive the economy in economic development and the type of work we do; we recognized and realized that the consumer markets, and the regulatory structure, are also a vital part of that dynamic. As we did this and we looked at a community, we learned there were certain things that didn't fit into those categories, such as traffic counts, congestion, and commute times. Public school grades, parks, open space aesthetics, and a sense of place that connects people to a place, which I'll tell you more about in a mo-ment.

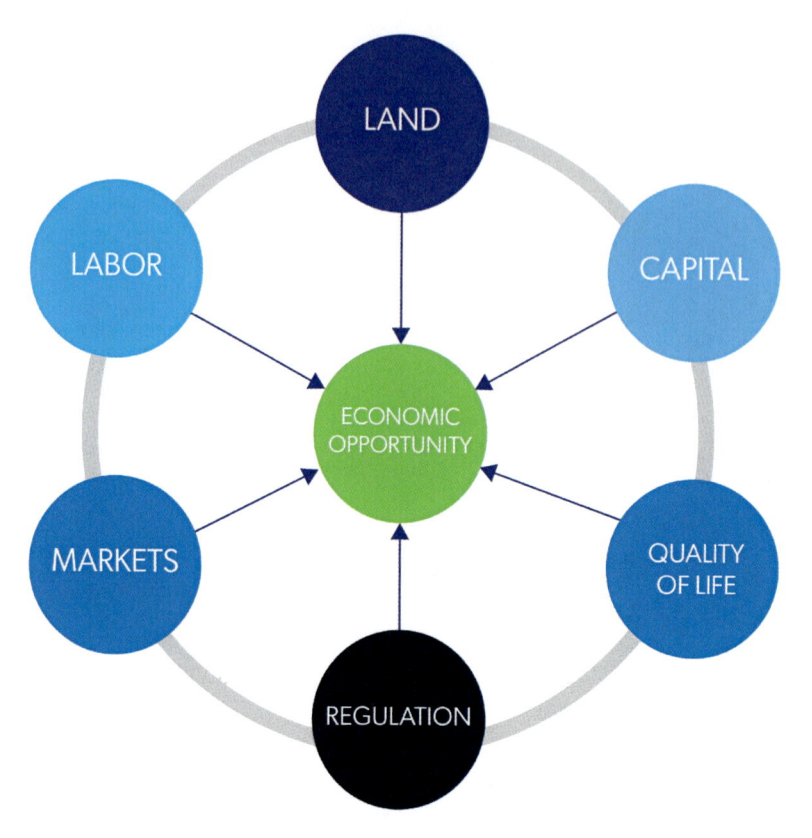

```
        LAND
LABOR          CAPITAL
   ECONOMIC
   OPPORTUNITY
MARKETS       QUALITY
              OF LIFE
      REGULATION
```

You don't have to have expensive data sets or deep access to data to know what's going on with each of these drivers in your community. The key is to understand what's happening with each of these drivers; more data can help you do that. But how it is applied is that you're going to look at the reality of each driver. They're going to say, what can we, the city, the main street, the convention bureau, or any of our other partners, what can we do realistically and within our resources and skills to positively influence each of these drivers to the better for the goal we're trying to accomplish?

So, if you think about Land, you know what's happening with the real estate in your community. You know whether or not the city or one of your partner organizations owns land that could be a catalyst. You know the properties for sale, those that just sold, or the vacant properties. So you can start with that. You don't even have to get into the rental rates and the trends and all of that; you need to get that sense of what's happening in your community.

Labor is a harder one to influence directly. You lack control over the labor markets at the local level. The best thing you can do is to do the quality life things that make your community a place people want to be, whether it's a place for talent, business and business owners and entrepreneurs, or both. But understanding commuting, inflow, and outflow helps.

An example is Tequesta, Florida, where we used cellphone data to understand what's going on with their workforce and with their residents who are in the workforce. So, to understand who's coming to the Village to work and where their residents are going. And this was important because we needed to understand this. After all, in early 2023, the Florida Department of Transportation (FDOT) shut down the US-1 bridge from Jupiter to Tequesta for 19 months to build a new bridge. So, we needed to understand this because we're looking at the impact on the businesses in Tequesta. But you know, anecdotally, you hear things, who's hiring, who's not hiring, who can't find staff, who can't find the talent they need, who can't find jobs. What sort of skills and training is required? So, what can we do with this, or what can one of our partners do to help this situation?

The third driver is Capital. Capital is money; we always need more to accomplish our goals. So it's trying to understand what's going on with capital for private investment and public investment. So, public investment is trying to find creative and broad sources of funding and financing for initiatives. Lots of infrastructure money out there

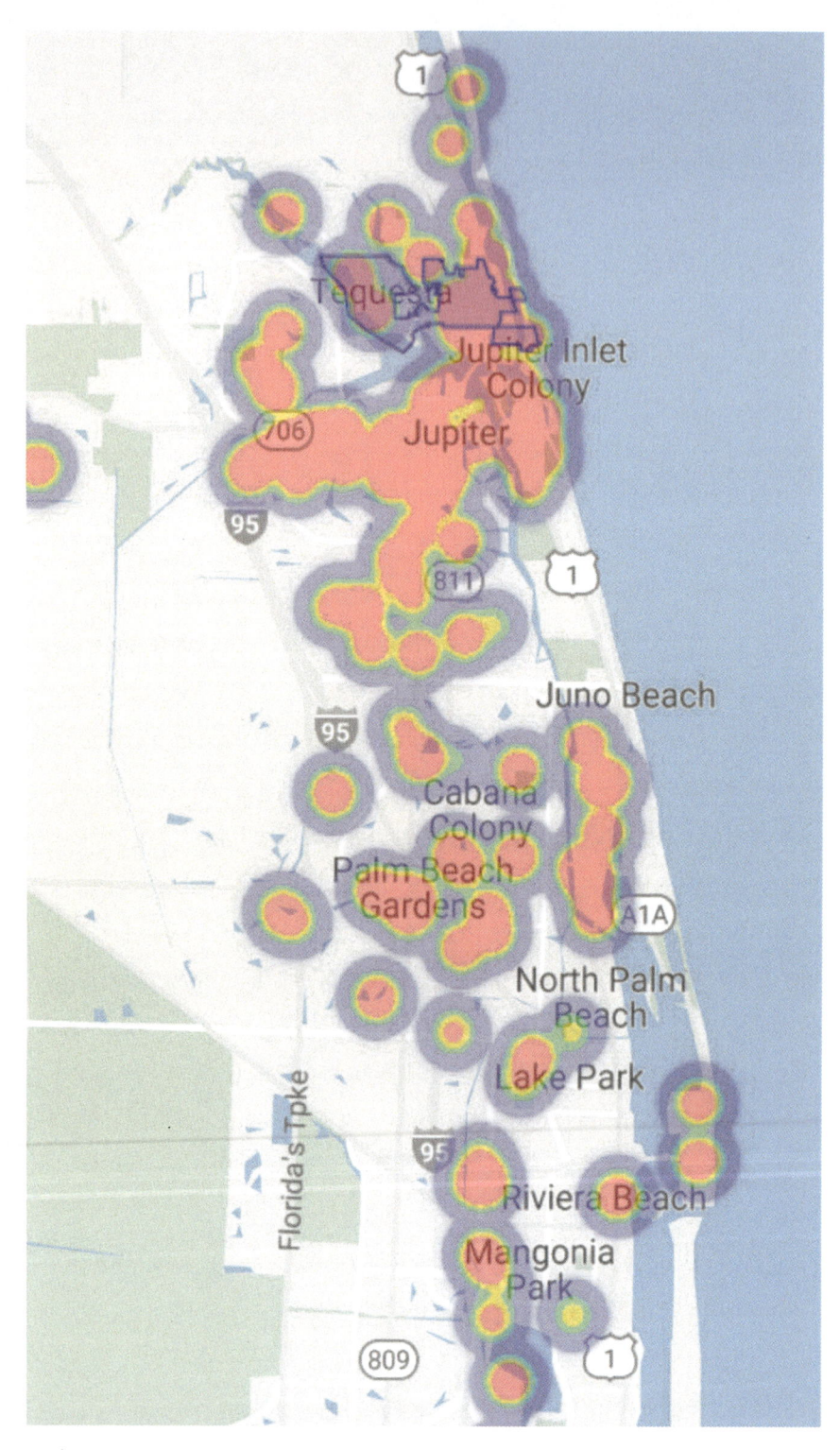

Tequesta, Florida resident labor shed. Source: Placer.ai

right now. Much money for resiliency projects, hardening, economic development, and different types of projects is available. There can be nuances to knowing how to rank and score on these and finding some of those hidden gems.

Looking at, sometimes, a private sector model and understanding what the assets are like when we look at projects, we don't value things like goodwill. So we just did this example in a South Florida redevelopment area, working for a developer who will do the infrastructure. He's building two significant projects in two different parts of the community, but he's building the infrastructure that connects them with that infrastructure. We looked at a model that looks at the additional investment they can spin off in those areas receiving infrastructure and the additional economic impact and increment revenue that type of investment can create.

Understanding what is going on in the private sector and what's going on with financing, we know right now, we know where rates are. We know where the rates are for buying homes or construction loans. We understand what inflation is doing to housing prices. And we know what's happened with development with the cost of con-struction, labor, and interest rates. What does that mean for what's feasible and realistic now, and also understanding the trends and where these might go so we can start planning to be ready at the right time?

Next is regulation. Regulation is where a city has more control and influence over an economic driver than anything else. But each community's ability to influence each of these will be different from

Miami Shores Neighborhood

the neighboring community, maybe even different in various neighborhoods in the community. But this is it. Are the regulations reasonable? Are they redevelopment or revitalization-friendly? Does nimbyism drive them? Is the application of the rules fair? Is the certainty and predictability built into the process, or is there a reputation for cronyism?

Even when you fix regulatory processes, the market may not believe it for a few years. When you have a community that may have some folks with deep pockets who don't want anything developed, they may be able to start litigation to stop things or slow them down. All of these go into the return on investment consideration, the risk profile, and the risk premium that investors will put into a potential deal in the community. Are there charter amendments that impact feasibility, such as a voter referendum for the lease of city property?

Quality of Life takes many forms. It is imperative that leaders understand the positive and negative elements that connect people to a place.

Quality of Life: this is the connection to the community. Again, economic development is all about creating places people want to be, where they want to live, where they want to work, where they want to open a business, where they want to renovate a historic building, where they wish to send their kids to school, where they want to attend an event in your downtown and where they want to be around other people.

4
Community Connections

But what are the three most important things that connect people to places? First are the aesthetics, the look and feel of a place. That is the number one thing discovered in what connects people to their community. Do your aesthetics deliver on your brand promise? For example, in Miami Shores, a very upscale, upper-income community in Miami Dade County, there are beautiful neighborhoods. But is their downtown delivering on that identity?

The second thing that connects people to the place are the social offerings, the activities, and the opportunities for people to gather and engage with one another. And those can happen in third places, such as breweries, coffee shops, bookstores, gyms, and even the parking lot of the Harley dealership or a Big Lots. I was in Belle Glade and didn't see a local gathering spot. In the end, I found it, and it was the parking lot of the Big Lots.

Third Places like breweries and coffee shops provide opportunities for people to engge with each other, better connecting them to their community.

This engagement can also happen in public-activated spaces—pocket parks, bandshells, bike trails, jogging trails, the beach, and the boardwalk. But the city has to make sure to activate these public spaces so they are open and welcoming. Building a bandshell but prioritizing revenue generation over activation does nothing to improve the desirability of a place.

The third thing that connects people to their community is how open and welcoming the community is. And that includes everything from the greeting when you sit down at the diner when you first roll into town to that experience when you walk into City Hall to the permit counter. So these are all quality of life things. These are your parks, traffic, commuting, parking problems, school grades, open space, connectivity, and recreation corridors, all of which contribute to the quality of life.

5
The Markets: Customers

The final investment driver is the Customer. The markets are where you start looking at demographics and where you start looking at spending. Now, one of the things you've probably all heard about is a gap analysis. We'll talk about that in just a moment.

But let's begin with your downtown. When we think about downtown, you know, the first thing is that downtowns are an essential part of the city because even when it's a larger city like Homestead, like Miami, like Orlando, or when it's a small town like Stuart, or Arcadia, your downtown is your primary place brand. It influences everything else regarding economic development that happens in your community. Understanding the role of downtown is critical and one that many economic developers need to pay attention to, especially if they only have a regional or statewide view, because those

Downtown Miami Shores

organizations are usually only focused on transactional economic development with its limitations.

So, your downtown customers, well, you have five ways to get them to come to you. Not all downtowns will have all five methods. You're going to have people who walk, you're going to have people who ride a bike to it. You're going to have people who take transit to it, which not everybody may have. You'll have people who take a ride share like Uber and Lyft to it, which, again, not everybody has. And you'll have people who drive to downtown.

In Miami Shores, we looked at two primary markets. People that live within a 15-minute walk or bike ride, and people within a five-minute drive. A five-minute drive encompasses the majority of the Village and a larger area. Downtown Miami Shores has 162,000 square feet of retail and 155,000 square feet of office space, but about 60 to 70,000 square feet are uses that should be off the ground floor, es-

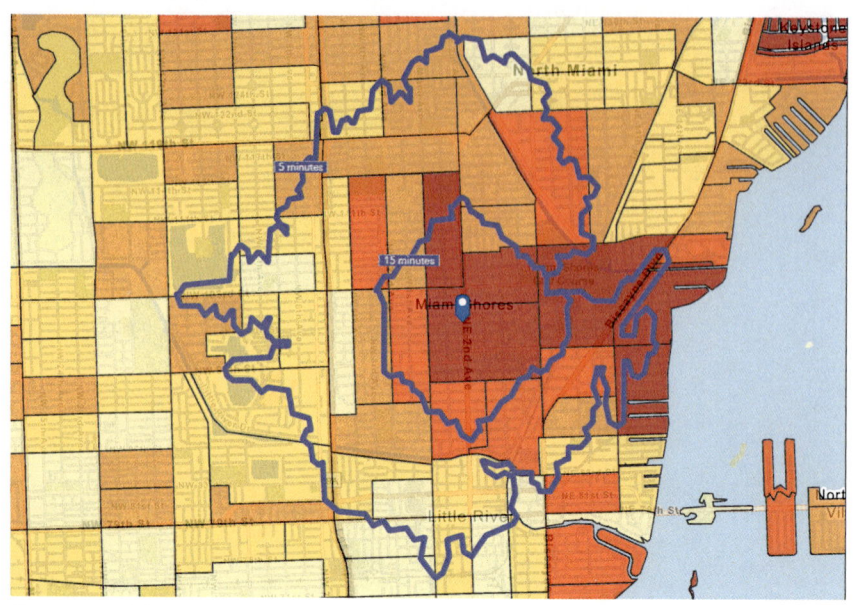

Downtown Miami Shores 15-minute walk and 5-minute drive time radii. ESRI.

pecially a lot of medical real estate offices and even some storage. But we do have a few restaurants.

The population within a 15-minute walk is 6,000, with a median household income of $122,000. When we looked at a five-minute drive, that population is 45,000, but the median income is only $52,000 annually. So, we moved on from traditional demographics to newer systems.

BusinessFlare® utilizes a service called Placer.ai, which was developed for retail and shopping centers using cell phone location data. We realized there were 1.5 million customer visits to downtown in the last year by customers and an additional 205,000 visits to downtown in the previous twelve months by the people who work downtown. We also determined that the 1.5 million customer visits were by 276,000 individuals. That is a more significant market area from the 45,000 who live within a five-minute drive or the 6,000 who live

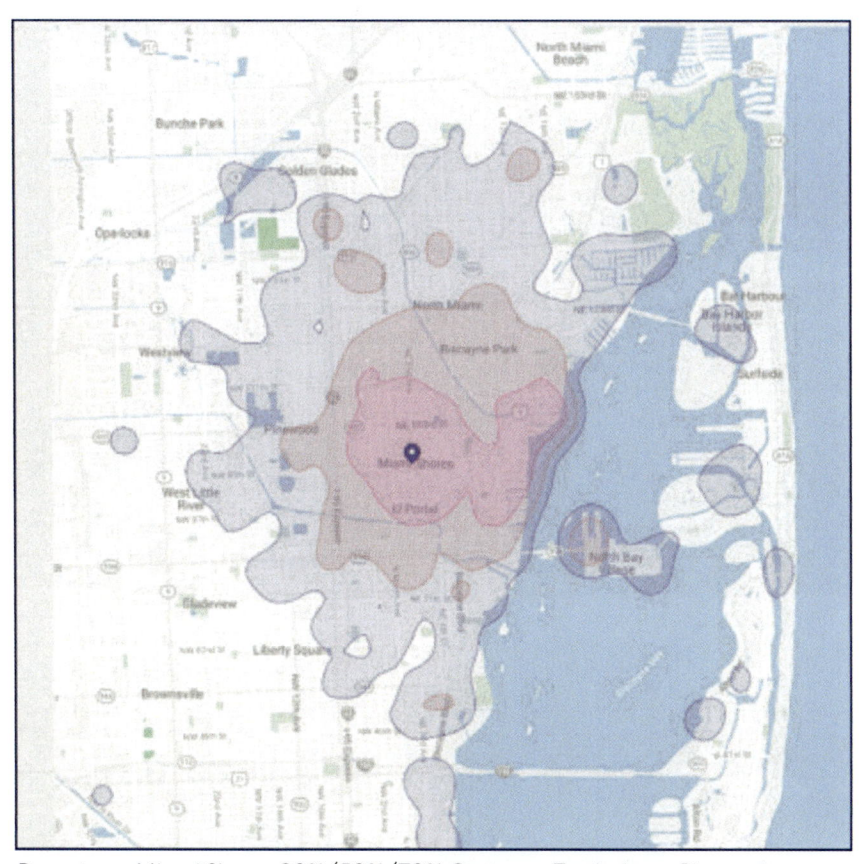

Downtown Miami Shores 30%/50%/70% Customer Trade Area. Placer.ai

within a 15-minute walk. It is an extensive trade area. But we also found that 13,000 people made 600,000 of those 1.5 million trips and that 142,000 people only came in once, and that one third of the customer visits were by people that live within one mile of downtown.

We discovered that out of these customers' favorite places, some places downtown were in their top preferences. One of the downtown gyms, as was the historic theater along with three restaurants in the same block. But then we said, well, let's look at just the residents; let's draw a geofence around the Village and see what the residents are doing and where the residents go. Those same three

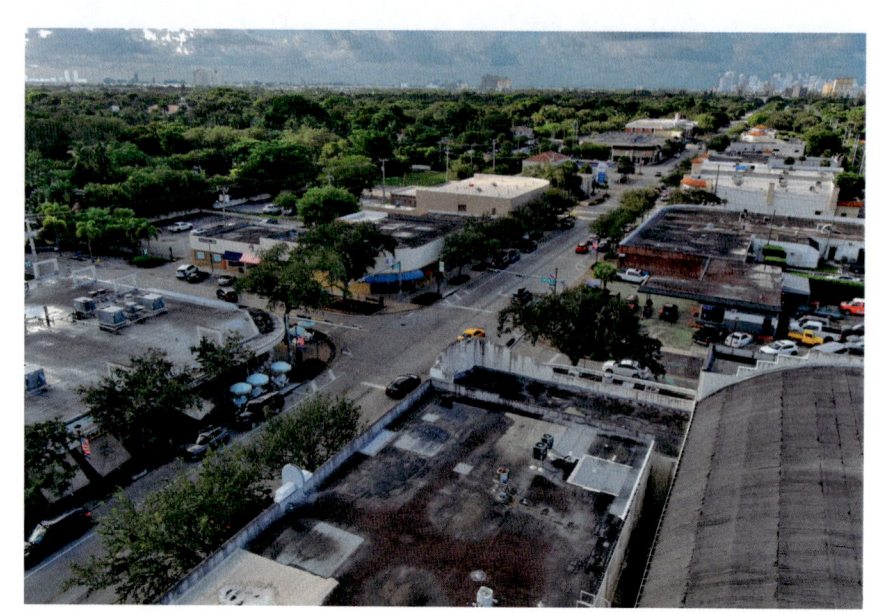

Downtown Miami Shores

restaurants were among their top 15, except they were ranked higher: number one, four, and six out of all the restaurants residents visited in the prior twelve months. Now, what else might be needed downtown?

6
Gap or Gut?

A gap analysis usually occurs when a consultant comes in and says, "Okay, this is your trade area. This is your market area. We have so many people in this market area who spend so much on these items. But within this area, there's this much in sales in here. So, in some things, there's more spent on groceries within this area than purchasing power. So, there is more capacity for another grocery store to be interested. But more can be spent on pharmacies, Walgreens, and CVS. So, there's additional spending potential in this trade area on pharmacies that is currently spent outside of the trade area, which means that in this trade area, we could support that dollar amount times the expected dollars per square foot in that type of establishment. So we can support another 7,500 square feet of that use downtown for example.

The problem is defining the trade areas, and that's something that's changed our approach with this new location data. That's one of the problems. The second problem with a gap analysis is the intangible of the entrepreneur. Say it says there's no additional spending pow-er for restaurants in my trade area. There's more already being spent here than spending power that could be more meaningful to me. If I'm just like Tony Goldman in South Beach, and I see the potential, know what I can do, and see the perfect building for it, gap analysis and unmet demand are meaningless. I can make this work and just have to bring their money to me instead of where it's going today. That's what I have to do. I have to create a place people want to be.

There is a great book that is relevant to creating the place people want to be over your competitors. It is called "Unreasonable Hospi-tality" by Will Guidara. He built a restaurant in New York City, Eleven Madison Park, that ultimately became the number-one restaurant in the world. His stories about the restaurant business are about places and "the remarkable power of giving more than they expect." I highly recommend you google "Will Guidara Hot Dog Story" to understand his experience in placemaking economic development fully and why stories are more important than numbers on a spreadsheet.

So, save time from overloading on things like gap and demand analysis. They will be meaningless to what you want to be or what you can be. Figure out what people want and give it to them: not just the product, but the experience. Then, please provide them with a place for what they want. And how are you going to do that? You're going to do that by telling stories.

The commonly understood type of gap analysis is insufficient as it only considers one factor and does not consider the intangible of the entrepreneur's potential. Many other factors affect a business's ability to serve all kinds of demand, and some businesses and entrepreneurs can compete and succeed in an oversupplied sector. Gap analysis occurs when a community's downtown offerings are often different from what people want. But true success lies in creating a place people want to be with what they want. That is the realm of the entrepreneur not the analyst. If downtowns do not have what people want, downtowns must figure out why people do not want to provide those things in their community.

Ultimately, successful economic development is an exercise in intestinal fortitude and not always a place to play it safe. Look beyond the trailing data and find your community's potential. Learn from successful entrepreneurs and apply their thinking to your economic growth efforts. Don't rely solely on the data; instead, eat a gut sandwich, which puts the relevant data between a slice of intuition and a slice of instinct.

7
Opportunities

Okay. So, back to South Beach and other places where we have worked with this approach. This approach came from how South Beach happened because we got many visits from communities in the late 90s and early 2000s wanting to know what the city had done. What was the plan? How did we do that level of revitalization? And the reality was that there wasn't a plan. It was organic and entrepreneurial. It was at points done without support and against the city's will, but eventually, the city got with the program and joined in.

But we needed to be able to answer this question for these communities that were coming and asking. And so we thought, what are the five most important things? What are the top five things that happened? So we attached a single word to each of the five, which became the approach we've worked with in many communities.

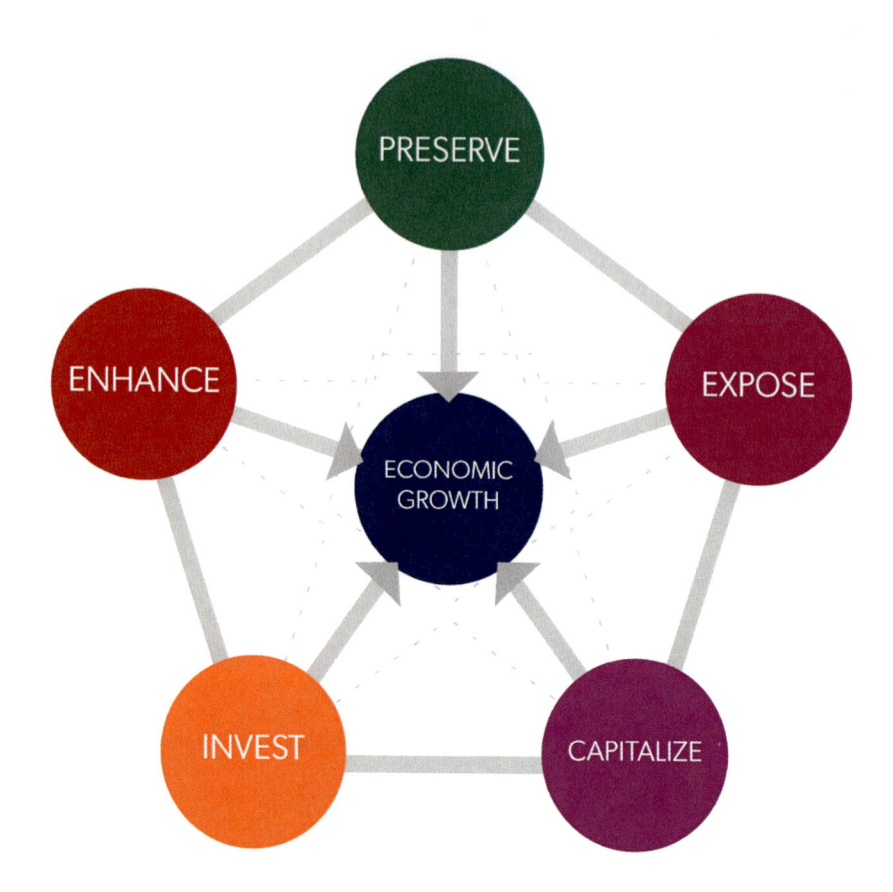

```
        PRESERVE

ENHANCE              EXPOSE

       ECONOMIC
        GROWTH

   INVEST      CAPITALIZE
```

It is a unique approach, and there is no wrong answer. It's excellent for consensus building because you often end up with concepts that many agree with. It's what's made some of the communities with a reputation for hostility and other challengs into some of our biggest successes.

This is because it's evident that we don't come in to tell the community what they should be. We find out what a community wants to be and perform a respectful reality check that lets them understand how to get there and work through this approach to help them see a realistic way to get where they want to go.

So we said well, what are the most important things that happened?

Applying the BusinessFlare® P.I.E.C.E. Approach during public engagement in Lake Park, Florida.

The historic house typology in West Coconut Grove, and the more recent "sugar cube" type of development, which pushes activity away from the neighborhood.

PRESERVE. The Art Deco Historic District was preserved as a local and National Register district. Buildings are sometimes the preservation answer in this approach, but not always, like in Martin County's Port Salerno neighborhood. There, it is about preserving that fisherman's village type of laid-back lifestyle that the people enjoy in that community. In West Coconut Grove, it was about protecting the cultural heritage from the history of the Bahamian community and their descendants, some of the first settlers in Miami who built that neighborhood and other parts of the city.

ENHANCE. The next thing that happened was a major beach nourishment project in the late 1970s and early 1980s. Widening the beach was an audacious enhancement in Miami Beach. In Palm Springs, enhancing the Village's place brand and identity was necessary to move forward with economic growth and to differentiate it

BusinessFlare® recently worked with the Village of Palm Springs, Florida to enhance their brand and marketing efforts.

Beachfly Brewing in Rockledge, Florida.

from other places in Palm Beach County. Additional enhancements can include regulatory enhancements that incorporate market and financial feasibility.

INVEST. Another thing that happened was investment. What is the critical investment to get to the next evolutionary step? Maybe a parking garage. In Miami Beach, it was a P3 with a parking garage providing Ocean Drive with additional public parking. However, this also offered new retail space in the historic district that led to the adaptive reuse of space buildings around it into fashion retail, which then created this connection over to Washington Avenue, which had just been nightclubs and ultimately led to the great streets of South Beach. In Rockledge, investment in the land and building across the street from their City Hall and Civic Hub enabled us to attract a brewery (Beachfly) while we were still designing, in what will one day be their downtown if leadership maintains its will.

CAPITALIZE. The next thing is, what can you capitalize on? In this example, rather than Miami Beach, the Downtown Miami Holiday

Inn provides a good example. I remember sitting at the Holiday Inn with someone working for the downtown organization and talking to either the proprietor, the bar manager, or the hotel manager. We noticed that the bar was quiet; there wasn't much going on. So my friend asked, what do you have that we could capitalize on and create some energy? He said, "Well, we have flight attendants"—light bulb on. Years later, that concept got me thinking about what one colleague taught me about downtown revitalization and real and perceived safety. He recently contributed a chapter to this book called "Design Downtown for Women, and the Men Will Follow"—light bulb on again.

Well, a recent example is what we needed to capitalize on in Groveland as we helped the CRA clean up their draft redevelopment plan; it was about capitalizing on FDOT's willingness to create this bypass to get all those trucks coming down State Road 50 out of the historic downtown.

EXPOSE. The final opportunity area is the most important. What can you expose? Expose is the storytelling. These are the most important stories, the hidden stories, the things that already exist and will make a difference if people can only learn about them.

And so again, this is about creating that place people want to be, and you're going to use some data to get there, but make sure you get relevant and meaningful data. You're gathering information. And that information doesn't always have to be data and numbers and spreadsheets. That's the point. But sometimes, the initial data can be a tour guide to find the hidden stories, like how researching occupational licenses in warehouses uncovers a common thread, which becomes a campaign that attracts what will ultimately be one of the largest and most successful craft breweries in the United States.

The Miami Beach example was a real exposure catalyst in the mid-1980s. Miami Vice exposed the world to Art Deco architecture with its pastel colors, followed by Bruce Weber's photoshoot for the original Calvin Klein Obsession campaign on the roof of the Breakwater Hotel. That memorable campaign exposed Miami Beach and those historic buildings, those art deco pastel buildings, to the world and turned our location into a visible film, fashion, supermodel, and celebrity hotspot, which in turn drove incredible tourism, entrepreneurship, and economic development.

In North Miami, we were working on an update to the redevelopment plan and an extension of the life of the redevelopment agency. As a musician, I knew what was there. There is this nondescript

The blue-gray building in the background is Criteria Studios, as seen from West Dixie Highway in North Miami, Florida.

building on West Dixie Highway that people drive by daily, but very few know what goes in there. It's situated behind this old American Legion. People move by, and they don't know what happens there. Even some of the local elected officials didn't know.

This building is one of American music history's most important recording studios. This authentic foundation makes it possible and accurate for the place brand for the development of a North Miami Music City effort. In North Miami, musicians can record, rehearse, buy equipment, have their gear serviced, and even teach at the School of Rock. But, save for a couple of small locations and periodic events, musicians must go somewhere else to perform to express their art. Art is created in North Miami, where the hidden music economy and infrastructure have existed for decades. Fleetwood Mac, Clapton, the Eagles, Aretha Franklin, the Allman Brothers and many more recorded here.

Some of the iconic American Music recorded in North Miami, Florida.

33

8

Economic Design™

The last thing I will leave you with before the stories is an approach we call Economic Design™. Planners come into communities, and they plan, and they write codes. And they draw pretty pictures. Economists and economic developers come into communities and give you many numbers, and they give you a thick market analysis with data you're never going to read. It overwhelms you, and they will tell you, here's all you can do. This is your demand, or lack of it, and you end up getting dollar stores, chains, and restaurants where the food comes out of a bag.

We start looking at opportunity sites and saying, okay, what can we do? What is this place's potential? At BusinessFlare® we have the benefit of understanding the ins and outs of development, finance,

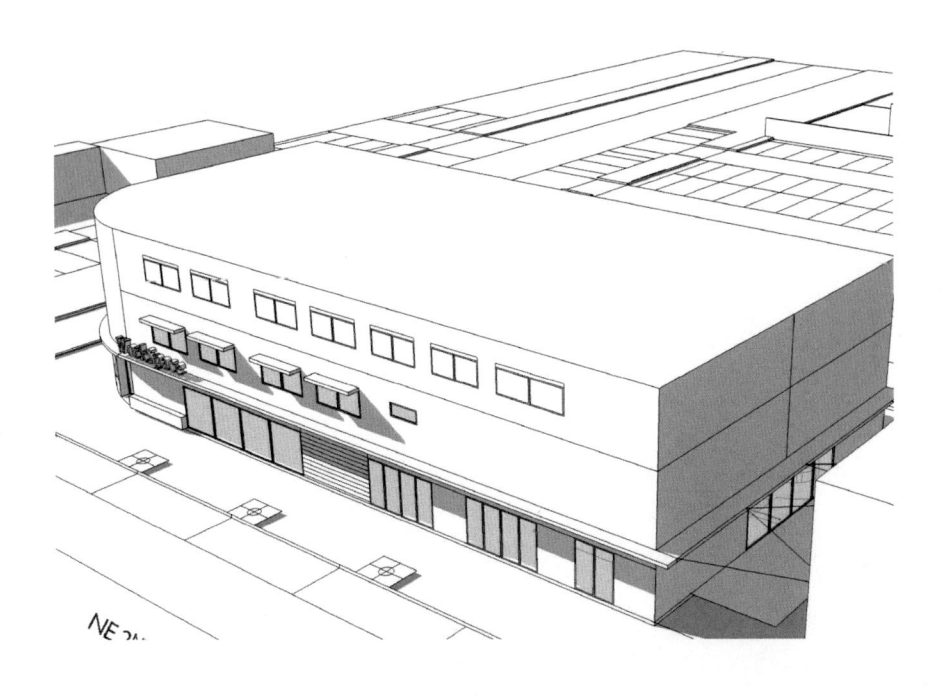

Fitment examples of different development scenarios for feasibility analysis of redevelopment of a Village-owned property in Miami Shores, Florida.

funding, and performance through our economic and fiscal impact analysis portfolio. So we sit with our in-house designer/ architect or an urban design partner as they draw and model different structure types and a range of other design elements, including zoning and development regulations.

We are simultaneously pro forma modeling and building all those variables into our economic model. All of the land use variables that they are working on. So if they changed parking requirements or minimum unit sizes or setbacks, that affects square feet, it reflects in our model, so we can look at what that does to an internal rate of return. We can look at what that does to the need to increase or the ability to decrease the incentive or other policy options. It lets us do sensitivity analysis for down payment assistance, publicly owned land, and purchase, lease, or all these different scenarios. It allows us to give, in this case, accurate data to the policymakers to understand the results of these different policy decisions.

	25% AFFORDABLE 80% AMI	25% AFFORDABLE 60% AMI	50% SUBSIDIZED 60% AND BELOW	50% WITH LAND 60% AND BELOW
DEVELOPMENT PROFILE				
Total Units	8	8	8	8
Affordable Units	2	2	4	4
DEVELOPMENT				
Land Acquisition	$500,000	$500,000	$500,000	$500,000
Construction	$1,029,000	$1,029,000	$1,029,000	$1,029,000
Soft Costs	$468,878	$468,878	$468,878	$468,878
Total Project Cost	$1,997,878	$1,997,878	$1,997,878	$1,997,878
Cost per Unit	$249,735	$249,735	$249,735	$249,735
OPERATING BUDGET				
Revenue	$156,843	$149,254	$122,202	$122,202
Expenses	$46,298	$46,298	$38,340	$46,298
Net Operating Income	$110,545	$102,956	$83,862	$75,904
RESERVES AND DEBT				
Replacement Reserve	$4,000	$4,000	$4,000	$4,000
Operating Reserve	$2,315	$2,315	$1,917	$2,315
Debt Service	$83,655	$83,655	$83,655	$83,655
Year 1 Net Cashflow	$20,575	$12,986	$(5,710)	$(14,066)
DEBT SERVICE				
Loan to Value	65%	65%	65%	65%
Loan Amount	$1,298,621	$1,298,621	$1,298,621	$1,298,621
Interest Rate	5.00%	5.00%	5.00%	5.00%
Annual Debt Service	$83,655	$83,655	$83,655	$83,655
CAPITAL STACK				
Debt	$1,298,621	$1,298,621	$1,298,621	$1,298,621
Impact Fee Waiver	$32,065	$32,065	$64,131	$64,131
CRA Grant	$0	$50,000	$300,000	$0
Other Assistance	$0	$0	$0	$0
Land Equity	$0	$0	$0	$500,000
Owner Equity	$667,192	$617,192	$335,127	$135,127
TAX INCREMENT RECAPTURE	$-	$100,502	$81,863	$-
INTERNAL RATE OF RETURN	11.2%	10.2%	8.9%	12.3%
Fiscal Impact				
Incentives	$32,065	$182,567	$445,993	$564,131
20-Year TIF to CRA	$324,226	$301,969	$245,966	$222,626

Excerps from the West Grove Housing Blueprint produced by BusinessFlare®, Plusurbia and Corradino, demonstrating the Economic Design™ methodology which merges design, land use, and financial feasibility to uncover all policy options and how they can work together.

9
Tell Your Stories

Storytelling. Every place has stories that no one knows. These stories need to be told. They tell the story of potential and opportunity, get people interested, and let you reveal more of these stories of potential. They make a real difference if people can hear them. It allows you to take investment drivers and those things that help you better position and understand how they can attract investment and entrepreneurs.

Stories are everywhere. We all have 1000s of them. And so do places. Every place has stories to tell, which are meaningful and relevant to economic development because they tell the story of the place. More importantly, they tell the story of the people of that place. And you learn so many cool things when you listen to people tell stories about themselves, their friends, their business, and their place.

Stories are how we uncover those hidden gems, and the core factor that makes a difference in economic development and helping create a place people want to be or helping make a great place that much more significant. People will want to be there; people will want to live there. Open a business, renovate a historic home, create an innovation, and rejuvenate.

So, what are the stories we look for? What captures the stories and exposes what is in this place? If people only knew it was there, it would make a huge difference in economic development and quality of life. Sometimes, the story doesn't have to be verbal or told in words. Sometimes, one image is all it takes. If you're one of the few lucky places, sometimes it's a TV show. Like what Miami Vice did, helping transform South Beach from God's Waiting Room and Wrinkle City into America's Riviera by exposing that historic architecture and those pastel colors in that beach setting. A more niche industry story is when Bruce Weber climbed on top of the Breakwater Hotel in Ocean Drive and shot the first Calvin Klein Obsession campaign. That black-and-white campaign exposed South Beach and the film and fashion opportunities to a broader part of that industry. It transformed it from European catalog shoots to celebrity central and attracted all the investment and entrepreneurship that followed.

Another example was the area Oakland Park hoped to become a downtown, which had all of these hidden uses in those light industrial warehouses that had something to do with the kitchen. An aspirational campaign branded the area as a culinary arts district. Exposing that connection to the kitchen led to the incredible Funky Buddha Brewery story, one of the nation's best brewery and economic development business stories. In North Miami sits a nondescript industrial building with no windows. Thousands of people drive by it every day. People who live there, elected officials from the area, may look past that old rundown American Legion hall and wonder what goes on in that building. Few realize it is one of American music history's three most important recording studios. Their first gold record was James Brown's "I Feel Good". Aretha recorded "Young Gifted and Black" there. It was the Bee Gees' home studio until they built their own. "Hotel California" and Fleetwood Mac "Rumours". Black Sabbath and Justin Bieber. Criteria is the studio where Tom Dowd brought Duane Allman in with Eric Clapton for the Derek and the Dominos recordings; they laid there.

But there's even more to expose once you expose that North Miami story. Musicians buy their gear not far down the street and down West Dixie Highway from that studio. Also, a couple blocks further is where musicians get their equipment serviced. Over by the studio are several groups of warehouses where another 12 or 13 studios have clustered. It is a place where musicians come and record. It's where musicians come and rehearse, and right around the corner is the School of Rock.

So, what needs to be exposed is not the celebrity and "cool" factor of Criteria Studios. What needs to be revealed is the soup-to-nuts music industry infrastructure that exists right there. Why does it need to be exposed? Because with all of that infrastructure, most of these musicians go somewhere else to express their art, and although there are limited opportunities in North Miami for musicians to express their art, North Miami truly is South Florida's Music City. There's a need for more locations, especially considering just how many venues Dade County has lost in the past several years. So, exposing this infrastructure creates the opportunity to rebuild the live music scene and to grow the part of that industry that is visible and helps create a place that people want to be: a proper music city for South Florida.

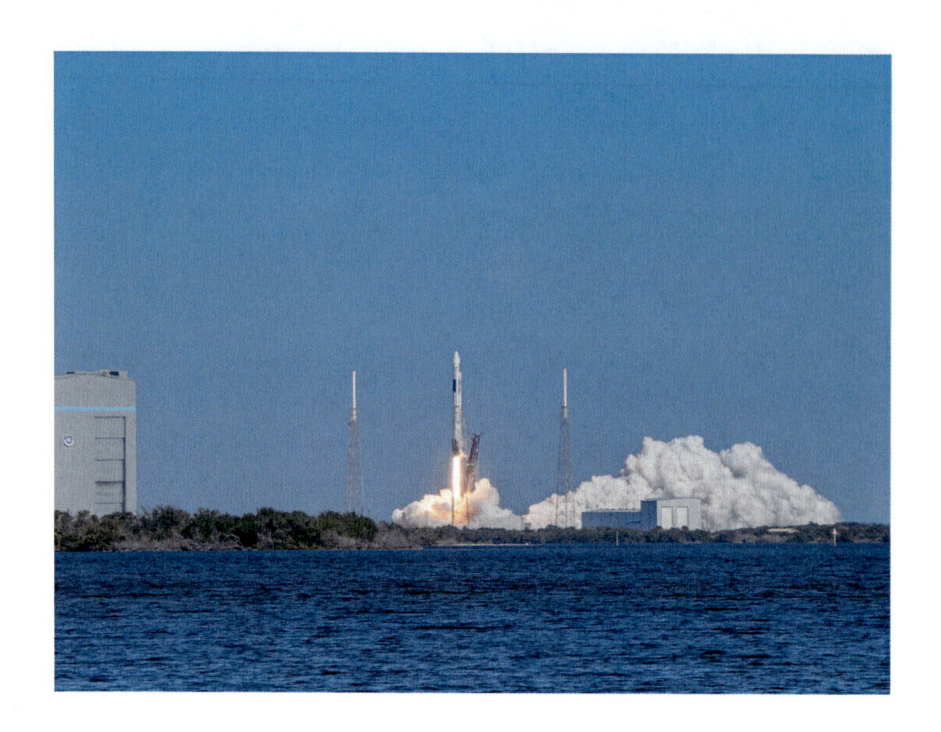

Up in Titusville, Palm Bay and Rockledge on the Space Coast, a lot is going on, and many exciting things are in the works. You don't have to expose what Elon Musk is doing and what Jeff Bezos and what the space industry and all of that is doing, but to expose that it's not just the space industry; there's a robust aerospace industry there with companies like Boeing and Embraer, and then, of course, you've got Harris Corporation down in Palm Bay, and many others.

But what does need to be exposed is that the need for talent creates such an excellent opportunity for the area's cities if they can find the will to create a place that talent wants to be. In this case, the twist is that the talent does not need the story. The talent knows the story of SpaceX and Blue Origin.

The Space Coast cities need to continue to hear the story, and hopefully, one of the cities will grab that entrepreneurial spirit and say we will be the place for this talent. Because right now, that's not where the talent is; many of them are only there to work, and the city that figures it out and finds the will to go all in on being the place for talent on the Space Coast will become the place that people want to be more than anywhere else in that area, and for everything else, not just space.

Over in Bradenton along MLK Boulevard, the story is about the history of that once thriving district. So, let's find the story of the businesses that were there. A review of the list of the historical black-owned businesses that once thrived in the area reveals a story that can inspire revitalization. Now, we can only partially replicate all those businesses; we won't find a financially feasible livery stable and an entrepreneur willing to invest in it.

But there was an ice cream shop, and there still is an ice cream shop. So, there is an excellent connection to the past to start the story. There were places for people's needs, such as tailors, places for entertainment, places to gather, places for food, and places for community, such as the churches that still exist. There were rooming houses, so we could still focus on places for people to stay, if in a different form. People wanted to be in this district, and they wanted to be in these places where the livery stable was a place for transportation. So let's get them a place for transportation.

Model of historic 9th Avenue in Bradenton. Family Heritage House Museum, Bradenton, Florida.

BLACK BUSINESSES OF YESTERYEAR

Bradenton, Florida

As we remembered Black Businesses on Central Avenue/ Ninth Avenue, currently called Martin Luther King's Blvd, from late 1920 through late 1980 by Caldonia M. Lewis and the late Buford Goodrum.

North side of the Avenue from Ninth Street West traveling East.

1. Webb's Rooming House--later 801 Bar
2. Epp's Rooming House--Later Minnte Archer Roominghouse; Royal-Cafe
3. Henry Burton's Tailor/Dry Cleaners
4. Pinky Livingston's Rooming House-Poolroom (Building called "The Stoneflat)
5. ncert Park Sunday Afternoon
6. ater Cab Stations (Randolph and Rowes)
7. Elder and Mack Sawyer (Brothers) Ice Cream Parlor, later Bartow's Cafe
8. Rooming House by George Bradley, later Ishman Chestnut
9. Harold Grant=Tailor Cleaners
10. Will and Mary Donovan's Livery Stable of Rented Horses and Carriages (Later called Stokes and Buster Mitchell's Gas Station and Auto Repair.)
11. Will and Mary Wade's Grocery (Later called Sonsy Williams Cab Station.)
12. Adam's Cemetery
13. Mt. Pleasant Methodist Episcopal Church (Later called Rogers Memorial and still later, Manatee Opportunity Council (MOC) and now the Martin Luther King Center.)
14. Home Smith and others Cleaners; (Later J. and J. Barbecue and A-1 Hair Salon.)
15. Rooming House--Ned and Lizzie Anderson Number 1

There are hidden stories that can make a difference. So, here are a few examples of how you start finding stories. Once you find one, you start pulling on the threads, and more stories emerge. They start weaving together into a story of entrepreneurship, success, opportunity, and potential. So, as you think about the stories from a new perspective of placemaking Economic Design™ rather than just stories of county and regional data, or stories just to enjoy around the table, find the right people in your places to tell these stories to and get to work.

ABOUT THE AUTHOR

Kevin Crowder is the founder of BusinessFlare®, an IEDC Certified Economic Developer, and an IEDC Certified Entrepreneurship Development Professional. Mr. Crowder has 30 years' experience implementing economic development, including 17 years as the Director of Economic Development and Government Affairs for the City of Miami Beach working out of the City Manager's office.

Kevin is a veteran of the U.S. Army, where he served in intelligence. His economic and impact analysis and experience give him a perspective that enables him to advise his public sector clients on actions that are realistic and attainable, including tactics to help grow the tax base and improve the client's economic development position.

He has led economic development planning and implementation in both public and private sector roles. He built one of the most robust municipal information gathering programs in the State of Florida for economic and market analysis to provide meaningful and relevant information to support investment and economic growth. He specializes in feasibility assessment and identifying policies, incentives and funding strategies to attract private business and investment, and his economic toolkit approach considers the ability of the individual local government to positively influence all of the drivers of investment.

He developed and implemented an innovative and effective approach to engagement, working with businesses, investors, developers, trade associations, business associations, and other stakeholders. Since establishing the BusinessFlare® brand in January 2013, Mr. Crowder has used the BusinessFlare® approach to help more than 60 communities improve their economic condition ranging in size from 1,500 to over 600,000, and in 2022 he performed economic and fiscal analysis on projects representing more than $5 billion in private sector investment in Florida.

Mr. Crowder can be reached at kevin@businessflare.net or 305.281.2279, and his Flareheads™ podcast can be found on all major podcast platforms and at www.flareheads.com.

www.businessflare.net
www.FloridaRedevelopment.com

ABOUT BUSINESSFLARE®

North Miami-based BusinessFlare® is an awesome collaborative enterprise that approaches Economic Design™ in a way that envisions each community's potential through a refreshing and unique experience based on authenticity, place brand and feasibility.

"We design economic spaces for everybody"

We specialize in all aspects of Economic Design™, with a focus on finding the right balance of economic feasibility, regulatory efficiency, and identity and place brand. We ground our work in a community's unique connection to its place: its aesthetics, social offerings, and openness. This framework allows us to develop strategic and tactical recommendations for successful implementation of actionable economic growth strategies. This is not pie-in-the-sky regional or transactional economic development; this is hands dirty, on-the-ground implementation of economic growth in real places.

We are an entrepreneurial team combines multiple disciplines into an approach that focuses on what makes a place the place that people want to be, with a realistic approach that understands market conditions, economics and design, regulation and policy, and local concerns and desires, and which respects every individual's perspective while providing a respectful reality check, especially on those things that are outside of a community's control but which can have an impact on your character and economy. We excel at all aspects of Economic Design™, and especially working with niche revitalization drivers like craft breweries, live music, and markets.

Our entrepreneurial approach has expanded our work into other states, gaining valuable experience in economic development approaches that are not as common in Florida, but which add value for our clients.

BusinessFlare® is a State of Florida Veteran and Minority Owned Business, which was founded and is led by Kevin Crowder, the former Economic Development Director for the City of Miami Beach and a Certified Economic Developer (CEcD) and Entrepreneurship Development Professional (EDP).

Made in United States
Orlando, FL
24 June 2024